P9-DEZ-417

Student Rights

DEBATING
THE ISSUES

Student Rights

mc Marshall Cavendish
Benchmark
New York

AUBREY HICKS

Library of Congress Cataloging-in-Publication Data
Hicks, Aubrey.
Student rights / Aubrey Hicks.
p. cm. — (Debating the issues)
Summary: "Examines the two sides of the debate related to freedom of speech and press, censorship, the right to protest, and the ability to practice freedom of expression and religion, and how it affects students today"—provided by the publisher.
Includes bibliographical references and index.
ISBN 978-0-7614-4969-0 (print)—ISBN 978-1-60870-663-1 (ebook)
1. Freedom of speech—United States. 2. Students—Civil rights—United States. 3. Students—Legal status, laws, etc.—United States. I. Title.
KF4770.H53 2012
342.7308'5—dc22
2010039514

Editor: Peter Mavrikis
Publisher: Michelle Bisson
Art Director: Anahid Hamparian
Series design by Sonia Chaghatzbanian

Photo research by Alison Morretta

Front cover: Sonda Dawes/The Image Works.
Associated Press: Marc Golden/The Gadsden Times, 32; Associated Press, 38; Mari Darr-Welch, 43; Scott Brunner/Bedford Times-Mail, 49; Margaret Croft/The News-Star, 52; Duncan Mansfield, 56; Bob Child, 58; Bruce Winter/The Express-Times, 61. **Corbis Images**: Bettmann Archive, 29. **Getty Images**: Phil Ashley, 1, 2-3, 4-5; Tomasz Tomaszewski/National Geographic, 6; Stock Montage, 13; Karen Bleier/AFP, 19; Library of Congress, 21; Bob Pool, 24; Bill Clark/Roll Call, 31; Gary Tramontina, 37; Justin Sullivan, 42; Ted Thai/Time Life Pictures, 46; Mark Leffingwell/AFP, 63. The Granger Collection: **The Granger Collection**, 27. **The Image Works**: Mary Evans Picture Library, 9; World History/Topham, 11; Sonda Dawes, 34; John Birdsall, 59. **Superstock**: Howard Pyle/Bridgeman Art Library, 15; Stock Connection, 16; Richard Cummins, 20; Image Source, 45; Blend Images, 66; John Giustina, 68.
Back cover: Vito Palmisano/Getty Images.

Printed in Malaysia (T)
135642

Table of Contents

In the United States, the First **Amendment** to the Constitution guarantees people the right to **free speech**. People have not always been guaranteed this right. Societies have struggled with the notion of **censorship** since ancient times. Historically, there has been a movement away from censorship and toward free speech. Yet even today, societies must work to find a balance between the rights of the individual and the rights of society as a whole—the rights of the many.

There have always been people who have said something that someone else did not want to hear. Often the solution to the problem these people presented was to arrest, to silence, or to censor them. For instance, the Athenian philosopher Socrates was arrested and sentenced to death in 399 BCE because the Athenian government thought that by teaching his students to question authority, he was corrupting them. People are still arrested for their ideas today, in the twenty-first century, in foreign countries and the United States alike.

Censorship has been a part of the human story since the beginning. What about free speech? Ancient Athens, where citizens were granted the right to express themselves, may have been the birthplace

On Independence Day, this boy rides a tricycle to celebrate the First Amendment.

of the idea of free speech. However, only adult men were considered citizens; women and children were not granted the same rights. Athenian free speech is not the same idea of free speech as understood by law today in the United States. In the ancient world, if a citizen spoke against the government, the punishment was death.

The freedoms enjoyed by the Athenian male citizens soon gave way to an increasingly strict sense of right and wrong as the ancient empires of Greece and Rome fell. Centuries of religious wars and territorial battles among the kings and queens of Europe brought about churches and governments that controlled their citizens by keeping them in a solid grasp. The **Inquisition** is one of the strongest examples of the pervasive control that governments and churches held during this period. Many Europeans in the thirteenth century lived in fear of

CHURCH PUNISHES GALILEO FOR OBSERVATION

Galileo (1564–1642), an Italian astronomer, claimed that Earth revolved around the sun. His support of the Copernican theory of the universe was based on his observations of the sky using a telescope. It was a sin to disagree with the Roman Catholic Church's belief that the sun revolved around Earth, and so Galileo was tried for **heresy** in 1633. He was found guilty and placed under house arrest and spent the last years of his life confined to his home. Today Galileo is known as the Father of Modern Science for the contributions he made to the development of what is known as the scientific method.

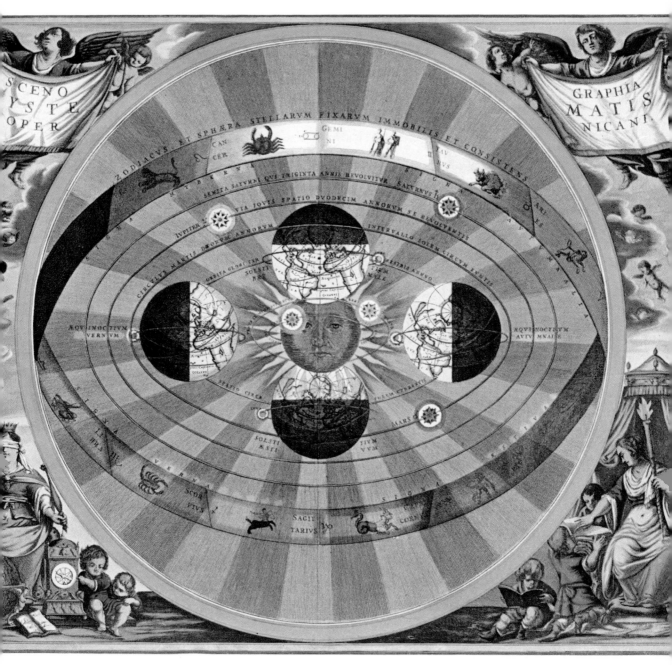

The Copernican theory that Earth revolved around the sun, shown in this illustration from 1660, was considered heresy by the Church.

the Grand Inquisitor. Even those who were faithful members of the Catholic Church treaded lightly when the Inquisition came near. Control over what individual people believed and said was a way to control the whole society.

Yet, during this era events took place that have echoed down through the centuries and led to the birth of free speech in the United States. Agreement was reached in England that would have far-reaching effects. King John was forced to sign the **Magna Carta** (Latin for "great charter") in the year 1215. England was in such strife thanks to King John's political mishandling and overtaxation of his people that he was forced to admit that law binds even the king. By attaching his seal to this document, King John agreed that the laws of the land would also bind future kings. The Magna Carta was the first document in European history to acknowledge that all free men possessed certain freedoms. It was this document from the Middle Ages that inspired the Founding Fathers of the United States to seek **redress** from the king of England. As English subjects, the freedoms written of in the Magna Carta would have pertained to them, including the right to fair taxation.

Though many **liberties** were mentioned in the Magna Carta, free speech was not among them. For much of the thirteenth through eighteenth centuries, debates about what men could say in public centered

DID YOU KNOW?

The Magna Carta is on display at the British Library in London.

THE SOCRATIC METHOD

The Athenian philosopher Socrates (c. 470–399 BCE), renowned as one of history's greatest thinkers, taught his students to ask questions and debate with their fellow students in order to promote clear thinking. Questioning and arguing were, to Socrates, an important part of the process of creating ideas and solutions to problems. Sometimes the best way to a solution is to find all the inferior solutions and explain why they do not work. At the age of seventy, Socrates was put on trial for corrupting the youth of Athens. He was found guilty, sentenced to death, and forced to drink poison.

Socrates is depicted as still arguing and discussing ideas as he is handed a cup of poison in this painting, *The Death of Socrates* by J. L. David in 1787.

INTELLECTUAL PROPERTY

Control of the printing presses during the thirteenth to eighteenth centuries was an entirely different matter from the control of speech. When a printer used his press to publish a document, it was his right to copy (**copyright**) the material. No one else, not even the author, had the right to print that material again without the printer's expressed permission. In 1710 authors were first given the right to copy material that they had written. Finally, an author was legally and for the first time in history recognized as the person with the right to copy. The idea that a writer "owned" his own writings was an important change in the thought about intellectual property. Individuals had more power over their own ideas thanks to this change. Power over one's own thoughts and ideas is central to the freedom-of-speech debate. It remains a hot topic of legal debate, even more so with all the new issues the rise of the Internet and digital media brings.

on **blasphemy**, or speech that went against church doctrines. Martin Luther, a German theologian, was excommunicated by the pope in 1521 for nailing his *Ninety-five Theses* to the church door at Wittenberg in 1517. His statement against the church's sale of indulgences began a debate within the church that led to the Reformation, a movement that resulted in the establishment of the Protestant churches. The split between the churches brought about even more religious intolerance as each sect wanted to silence the other.

Freedom of Speech in the United States

Though religious intolerance in England was a driving force for much of the immigration to the New World, intolerance followed the Pilgrims to the colonies. Puritans in Massachusetts drove out Quakers and people from other religious sects deemed heretical. There were even a

Martin Luther's writing sparked dissent within Christian churches that gave rise to a movement called the Reformation.

few cases, such as the Salem witch trials, that resulted in executions. In the colonies, there were steep punishments made upon those who spoke or acted against the established church of the region. Religious freedom and freedom of speech in the colonies was not guaranteed. The struggle to survive and build communities in the new land kept people both busy and afraid for the future. In fact, in most colonies it was the duty of the leadership to provide strong religious teachings in order to keep everyone on the straight-and-narrow path. In England the clergy and Parliament held the power. This model of leadership was brought to the colonies.

As the population of the colonies grew, so did the number of people who held positions of power. First, only government officials and clergymen could freely speak in public. As the local governments grew, so did the number of public officials who could speak without censure. A group of such government officials, using the Magna Carta as inspiration, wrote the **Declaration of Independence**, the **Constitution**, and the **Bill of Rights**. These three documents form the backbone of the American legal system, and, at least in theory, all debate regarding specific freedoms must go back to the words written on these pages.

DID YOU KNOW?

In the Maryland colony, those caught speaking against the Church had their property seized by the state.

In 1660 several Quakers, including Mary Dyer depicted here in *Mary Dyer on Her Way to the Scaffold*, a 1906 painting by Howard Pyle, were hanged for defying Puritan laws which forbade Quakers from living in the Massachusetts Bay Colony.

This depiction of the signing of the United States Constitution hangs inside the Capitol in Washington, D.C.

16

The Constitution and the Bill of Rights

Delegates from the colonies met in Philadelphia, Pennsylvania, on May 25, 1787, to draft the Constitution. Since the colonies separated from the British crown in 1776, the government had been acting under the Articles of Confederation. This meeting of delegates has become known as the Constitutional Convention. It took thirty-nine delegates four months to shape the new government of the United States of America. The first three articles of the Constitution created the three branches of government. Article four specifies that each state shall have a **republican** form of government. Article five addresses the question of future amendments to the Constitution. Article six declares the Constitution the supreme law of the land. The seventh article describes the requirements for **ratification** of the Constitution.

DID YOU KNOW?

The division and separation of power among three branches— legislative, executive, and judicial—created a system in which the parts checked and balanced each other. In a departure from the British system, in which all legislative and executive authority had come to reside in a single body, Parliament, the Constitution created a government whose powers were theoretically limited by the founding document itself.

The First Amendment

While the delegates knew it would be necessary to create a bill of rights, they put this task off until such time as the First Congress was elected. At the urging of Thomas Jefferson, the primary author of the Declaration of Independence, James Madison brought a draft for twelve amendments to a congressional committee in 1789. Ten of his original twelve were promptly ratified by the states, including the First Amendment, which guaranteed the citizens of the United States freedoms that far outshone the freedoms granted by governments of the past. The First Amendment reads as follows:

> Congress shall make no law respecting an establishment of religion, or prohibiting the free exercise thereof; or abridging the freedom of speech, or of the press; or the right of the people peaceably to assemble, and to petition the government for a redress of grievances.

Adoption of the Constitution and the Bill of Rights was the culmination of many years of struggle for individual rights and democracy. The trio of documents created a government in which the people could and should participate. The citizens of the original states took a chance on themselves in order to create a country that would be better for themselves and for future generations.

Despite the promise of the new government, disputes developed over the course of two and a half centuries that impact citizens today.

THOMAS JEFFERSON

A great believer in states' rights, religious rights, and freedom of the press, Thomas Jefferson was astounded when he tried to get a copy of a French scientific treatise only to find it censored by the state. He wrote, "Is this then our freedom of religion? And are we to have a censor whose imprimatur shall say what books may be sold, and what we may buy: And who is thus to dogmatize religious opinions for our citizens? Whose foot is to be the measure to which ours are all to be cut or stretched?" (quoted in *Freedom of Speech in the United States* by Thomas L. Tedford and Dale A. Herbeck).

Jefferson was the primary author of the Declaration of Independence and became the new country's third president.

Jefferson Memorial in Washington, D.C.

> **CONGRESS SHALL MAKE NO LAW** *respecting an establishment of religion, or prohibiting the free exercise thereof; or abridging the freedom of speech, or of the press; or the right of the people peaceably to assemble, and to petition the Government for a redress of grievances.*
>
> **❧ THE FIRST AMENDMENT TO THE U.S. CONSTITUTION**
> **15 DECEMBER 1791**

The text of the First Amendment is memorialized in Independence National Historical Park, Philadelphia, Pennsylvania.

Some disputes involve the question of which people are citizens with the inalienable rights granted by the Declaration of Independence. Over the centuries, minorities and women have attained these rights but not without cost. The Civil War was a test of the right for people to speak out on the abolition of slavery. The **civil rights** movement was a test for the rights of blacks and other people of color to obtain equal rights with those of whites. The feminist movement tested the rights granted to women against those already guaranteed to men.

Today there remains debate over what writings and oration are protected and what should be censored for the public good. When President William McKinley, the twenty-fifth president of the

Over 7,000 men died at the Battle of Gettysburg in 1863. President Abraham Lincoln's speech, known as the Gettysburg Address and depicted above, is remembered as one of the most important speeches in American history.

> # DID YOU KNOW?
> An editorial published shortly after President McKinley's death stated that the advocacy of anarchy is a crime and every speech calling for destruction of government should be followed by imprisonment.

United States, was assassinated in 1901, many states agreed that advocating or inciting a crime is illegal and not protected under the First Amendment. What society deems as inciting crime has changed over the course of the last century. For the first part of the twentieth century, prayer in schools was considered important to combating "moral anarchy." Today, the question of prayer in schools centers less on the idea of moral certainty and more on the idea of people's right to worship as they see fit. Change was and remains difficult to manage gracefully.

The system that the Founding Fathers laid out allowed for change through amendment, in the sense that all twenty-seven amendments are additions to the rules. So just as the First Amendment was an addition to the rules set forth in the Constitution, the basis for law may be regarded as still changing in accord with the popular will.

WHAT DO YOU THINK?

Is the United States the only country where citizens have the right to freedom of speech? Can you think of other countries that ensure their citizens the freedom of speech? How about countries that prohibit this First Amendment right?

What are the five freedoms protected under the First Amendment?

What rights did colonial Americans have? Were the rights different or the same in all thirteen colonies?

What does it mean to be able to "petition the government for a redress of grievances"?

Do you think there should be limits on a person's right to free speech? If so, what are the limits, and why should they be imposed?

Chapter 2

Judging the rights of minors is one of the more difficult questions facing courts, other institutions, and society as a whole today. Balancing minors' rights with the rights and wishes of parents makes the issue even more complicated.

Public schools are charged with teaching students to be good citizens. Whether the purposes of schooling extend beyond teaching students the rights of citizenship to according them the full rights of adult citizens is a hotly debated matter. There are many issues that administrators must take into account that might limit a student's actions or speech in order to protect others. The question remains, is it appropriate for minors ever to have the full protection of the First Amendment, and if so, when?

Out of the hundreds of cases that have been brought to court in the last fifty years, four stand out to summarize the direction that the courts have been headed when deciding the First Amendment rights of students. In the first case, a group of students in Iowa were suspended for wearing armbands to protest the Vietnam War. In the second, a young man was suspended for a graphic speech made during an assembly. In the third, a school newspaper was censored by the administration.

The highest court in the United States judicial system is the U.S. Supreme Court, housed in this building in Washington, D.C.

In the last, a sign advocating illegal drug use displayed off school grounds was cause for suspension.

Why Are These Cases Important?

The U.S. legal system was built upon the Constitution, which was designed to allow for modification when it was thought appropriate. American law is case law. That is, decisions made by state and federal courts become part of the legislative structure and can then be used by lawyers to argue the merits of new cases. When courts make similar decisions time and time again across the country, it becomes accepted practice. If the courts decide that school officials must prove that a disruption of education exists before students can be expelled, these court rulings affect school policies all over the country.

TINKER V. DES MOINES INDEPENDENT COMMUNITY SCHOOL DISTRICT

In 1965, President Lyndon B. Johnson was expanding and escalating the ground war in Vietnam. At home, the antiwar movement was beginning to reach proportions never before seen in this country. In November 1965, forty thousand protestors marched on Washington, D.C., calling for an end to the war. Just one month later, three students, John and Mary Beth Tinker and Christopher Eckhardt, in an Iowa public school decided to wear black armbands as a silent protest against the war. School officials suspended the student protesters. The Iowa

Civil Liberties Union (ICLU) helped the Tinker family file a lawsuit against the school. The suit claimed that the school violated the stu-

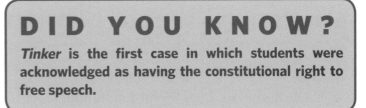

DID YOU KNOW?

Tinker is the first case in which students were acknowledged as having the constitutional right to free speech.

dents' First Amendment rights. The case went through several lower-court decisions and appeals before it reached the Supreme Court in November 1968. Justice Abe Fortas summarized the Court's decision: "It can hardly be argued that either students or teachers shed their constitutional rights to freedom of speech or expression at the schoolhouse gate." The Tinkers had won their case, and the decision of the Court affected First Amendment cases for several decades.

Mary Beth and John Tinker, along with their parents, brought a case against their school district that would change the way the law viewed student rights in the United States.

27

BETHEL SCHOOL DISTRICT V. FRASER

Matthew Fraser gave a speech to his 1983 senior class, in which he nominated his friend for student body vice president. His speech was filled with sexual innuendo and elicited several different reactions from the audience of six hundred students. Teachers had told him before the speech was given that it was inappropriate and must be changed. Fraser was suspended for three days for violation of the school code of conduct, which prohibited the use of profane or obscene language. His name was also taken off the list of students who would be eligible to speak at the graduation ceremonies at the end of the year.

With the help of the American Civil Liberties Union (ACLU), Fraser and his parents sued his school district for violation of his First Amendment rights. Like *Tinker*, this case was argued at several lower courts and appealed several times before it reached the Supreme Court in 1986. In writing the decision of the majority (7–2), Chief Justice Warren Burger wrote, "The First Amendment does not prevent the school officials from determining that to permit a vulgar and lewd speech such as respondent's would undermine the school's basic educational mission." In other words, it was the majority's opinion that **vulgar** and **lewd** language in schools was not protected by the First Amendment. School officials did have the right to punish Matthew Fraser for disrupting the assembly with his use of sexually explicit language.

HAZELWOOD SCHOOL DISTRICT V. KUHLMEIER

Former students of a journalism class in the Hazelwood School District, in St. Louis County, Missouri, sued the district for violation of their First Amendment rights. The *Spectrum* was a school-sponsored newspaper

Principal Robert Reynolds holds a copy of the *Spectrum* after the U.S. Supreme Court upheld his decision to censor student articles.

at Hazelwood East High School. As part of a journalism class, students would write articles for publication in the *Spectrum*. In 1983, Cathy Kuhlmeier and two other students claimed that the principal, Robert Reynolds, violated the sanctity of freedom of the press by deleting two of their articles from the paper. Reynolds argued that the material was inappropriate for some of the younger students at the school. The first article was about the effect of pregnancy on a student's life. The principal felt that even though the student's name was not mentioned, it could be inferred from the rest of the article and was therefore not appropriate for a school paper. The second article was about the effect of divorce on a particular student. The principal felt that the article was not objective journalism because the author had not interviewed the parents of the student. The Supreme Court ruled that the newspaper was not a public **forum** since it was part of the journalism curriculum of the school. Therefore, the principal was well within rights to censor material printed in the paper. The Court ruled that school administrators controlled school-sponsored activities, including newspapers.

MORSE V. FREDERICK

This case created an important distinction for courts deciding First Amendment cases involving students. Students from the Juneau-Douglas High School in Juneau, Alaska, were released from class to witness the passing of the Olympic torch during the 2002 Olympic Torch Relay. As camera crews were rolling, student Joseph Frederick unfurled a banner that read "Bong Hits 4 Jesus." Deborah Morse, the school principal, confiscated the banner and suspended the eighteen-year-old student. The distinction in this case is that while this was a school-sanctioned event, Frederick's banner was displayed off campus. The court's decision expands the rulings from *Tinker* by including all school-sanctioned events and any disruption of students that may affect the school. Ruling that because the sign supported the use of an illegal drug in a place where other students could read the sign, the school was not in violation of Frederick's First Amendment rights.

Students protest in front of the U.S. Supreme Court Building in Washington, D.C., during the trial of *Morse v. Frederick*.

Students, as minors, have only as recently as 1965 been granted recognition by the courts as having protection under the First Amendment. As these four landmark cases demonstrate, protection under the First Amendment is afforded to students only when their words or symbolic expression do not disrupt the class or affect classmates adversely.

Banned Book Week display in the Gadsden Public Library in Gadsden, Alabama.

WHAT DO YOU THINK?

Do you have a clear idea of what "offensive speech" is? Do you think it belongs in the classroom?

Who should get to decide what is vulgar and what is not? Can people have differing opinions as to what is vulgar?

Why is disrupting a classroom with bad behavior harmful?

How do you feel about having restrictions placed on the topic of a paper you write for class?

Chapter 3

The U.S. Constitution embodies the basic principles and laws of the United States and guarantees certain rights to its citizens. One could argue that good citizens play an active role in community and government affairs. One of the objectives of schooling is to instruct children in the responsibilities of law-abiding adults. Some believe that students should always be given the right to free expression since it is within the framework of the laws they will need to learn to live with as adults once outside the schoolhouse gates. Students have the same rights to life, liberty, and the pursuit of happiness as do adults. They should be protected under the First Amendment in the same way as adults.

This debate concerns only public schools, as private, non-taxpayer-supported schools are exempt from freedom-of-speech **obstruction**.

Free Speech and a Free Press

"It can hardly be argued that either students or teachers shed their constitutional rights to freedom of speech or expression at the schoolhouse gate."   —Justice Abe Fortas, in the Supreme Court decision
in *Tinker v. Des Moines* (1969)

Is this defaced Stop sign marked up with graffiti or street art?

According to the Supreme Court decision in *Tinker v. Des Moines Independent Community School District*, student expression could be limited only if it would generate substantial disruption in the classroom. The school administrators were unable to convince a majority on the Court that a few teenagers wearing black armbands with peace symbols would be disruptive to the classroom.

John Tinker (fifteen years old), Mary Beth Tinker (twelve years old), and Christopher Eckhardt (sixteen years old) decided to disobey the school board's decision to ban protest activities. They wore black armbands decorated with peace symbols to class to demonstrate their opposition to the Vietnam War. Supported by the Iowa chapter of the American Civil Liberties Union, the families petitioned the court for violation of First Amendment rights. The lower courts debated whether the wearing of armbands was even eligible for protection under the First Amendment. The Supreme Court decided that armbands are **symbolic expression**, and therefore wearing an armband was indeed protected under the rule of law. The courts also had to decide whether the school administrators had a valid reason for suspending the students. Did the fact that John, Mary Beth, and Christopher wore armbands create disorder in the classroom? Did their armbands infringe on the rights of others in the school?

According to a Supreme Court majority, the answer to those questions was no. Mary Beth did not substantially disrupt her classroom by wearing an armband. John did not invade other students' rights by wearing an armband. According to the decision, when all three were

AMERICAN CIVIL LIBERTIES UNION

Founded in 1920, the American Civil Liberties Union (ACLU) has described itself as working to support the individual's rights, that is, those guaranteed by the Constitution and the laws of the United States. The ACLU is a national nonprofit organization that focuses on providing legal help to those people whose liberties may be at risk (it has local offices in every state). It strives to protect each and every person, from students to individuals convicted of committing a crime. Groups that have opposed the ACLU include various religious groups, the American Legion (a veterans' organization), and the Boy Scouts of America—though not all for the same reasons.

A Christian organization protests the ACLU after a monument of the Ten Commandments is removed from a public building.

punished, the school had violated their First Amendment rights. In this case, the school district was in the wrong.

For the first time in history, public school students were given basic free speech protection by a court of law. According to the ruling, officials cannot censor any student if the student is not disrupting the class or infringing the rights of others. This was the first court ruling of its kind. At this time in American history, most states still had no corporal punishment restrictions. Students had a very limited set of expectations regarding their rights in school. It seemed that minors would follow other groups of the 1960s. Women and African Americans were slowly gaining more equality. **Jim Crow laws** were being abolished all over the country, and women were gaining more equality in the workforce and in their personal lives.

When segregation in schools first ended, many African American students walked to school under military escort to protect them from violent protestors.

DID YOU KNOW?

As of 2011, only thirty-one states banned the use of corporal punishment in public schools. The first state to adopt anti-corporal-punishment laws was New Jersey, in 1867. The last to adopt such laws was New Mexico, in 2011.

Since the *Tinker* decision in 1969, court decisions concerning students' protection under the First Amendment have gone both ways. One that student rights' advocates considered a setback was the *Hazelwood* decision of 1988. The courts upheld the school's decision to censor a student journalist's story. The majority of the Supreme Court Justices decided not to grant the student the same protection under the First Amendment as adult journalists. Not all court officials agreed with the majority vote in the *Hazelwood* case. In his dissenting opinion of *Hazelwood*, Justice William Brennan wrote that the *Spectrum* as "a student-press publication, accepts all rights implied by the First Amendment." While his argument was in the minority, it remains valid and is still argued today in court cases involving student-run papers. In fact, some states have passed laws granting students stronger protection under the First Amendment.

No Disruption, No Problem

In *Dean v. Utica Community,* 2004, a federal district court judge ruled in favor of Katy Dean, a student journalist in Utica, Michigan when her article was censored by the principal. Dean received a tip about a lawsuit against the school district brought by local man; his suit **alleged** that the carcinogenic fumes of the buses idling for hours near his home had caused his lung cancer. Dean's article included information about the connection between diesel fumes and cancer. When she tried to contact school officials in connection with the lawsuit, their response was, "No comment." When her article was pulled from the paper by the principal, Dean and her mother sued the school district for violation of her First Amendment rights. The court ruled that the censorship had no educational merit. Judge Arthur Tarrow quoted President Dwight D. Eisenhower in his decision: "Don't join the book burners. Don't think you are going to conceal thoughts by concealing evidence that they ever existed."

A school fails its students when it cannot teach them the responsibilities of citizenship. They cannot operate as responsible citizens if they are not given the rights of citizenship. One of the tenets of the First Amendment is the protection of a free press. If the articles did not create a disruption in the classroom and if the articles did not infringe on any one person's rights, they should have been protected under the First Amendment.

DID YOU KNOW?

The Supreme Court of the United States is the highest court in the country and is made up of nine justices including one chief justice and eight associate justices. Supreme court justices are appointed by the President but must be approved by the Senate.

The Constitution states that it surpasses all other laws. If school students are considered citizens and public schools teach children to be good citizens, then the rights of the First Amendment should apply to students. Journalists writing for school newspapers should have the right to a free press. As Justice Brennan said of the expectations of the students at Hazelwood, "The young men and women of Hazelwood East expected a **civics** lesson, but not the one the Court teaches them today." Following the decision of *Hazelwood*, there was an increased effort by administrators to censor student newspapers across the country. This decision affected plays and other expressive activities within schools as well as school newspapers.

If the students wrote, produced, and distributed a paper off campus without any help or permission from a school official, they would have protection of the First Amendment. Once inside the school, however, the students lose that protection.

Personal Is Political

In late 2008, the Grossmont Union High School District in San Diego County reversed its decision to censor students wearing buttons and T-shirts expressing their opinion of **Proposition** 8 in California.

A similar case in Florida, 2007–2008, centered on a student, Jane Doe, who was being harassed because of her sexual orientation. When she complained of the harassment to Principal David Davis of Ponce de Leon High School, he told her that homosexuality is wrong and that if there was any further trouble, she would be suspended.

PROPOSITION 8

Proposition 8 appeared on the California ballot in the 2008 election. It proposed changing the state's constitution to limit marriage to partnerships between a man and a woman. The proposition was passed, and the following article was added to the California state constitution: "Only marriage between a man and a woman is valid or recognized in California." The controversy did not end with that vote. The central question regarding this ballot is whether majority rule can outweigh the rights of individual freedoms. On August 4, 2010, a federal judge overturned the vote. In his decision, Justice Walker said that Proposition 8 "fails to advance any rational basis in singling out gay men and lesbians for denial of a marriage license."

Buttons to protest Prop 8.

Several of the girl's friends, including eleventh grade student Heather Gillman, responded by wearing T-shirts with the words Gay Pride on them or by writing GP on their bodies in support of their friend. The principal decided that the wearing of T-shirts expressing support of homosexuality would be banned and the students would all attend a mandatory "morality assembly." On November 2, 2007, Heather and her parents wrote a letter to the school board asking that they look into the situation as they felt the principal had violated the students' right to free speech.

Heather Gillman's right to symbolic expression was upheld by the courts.

When the school board dismissed the letter, Heather and her parents sued the school district and the principal for violation of Heather's First Amendment rights. Federal Judge Richard Smoak ruled in favor of the students in the court findings in the case *Gillman v. School Board for Holmes County Florida et al* in July 2008. His order read, in part, "The School Board for Holmes County, Florida, shall take such affirmative steps as are necessary to remedy the past restraints of expression of support for the respect, equal treatment, and acceptance of homosexuals."

Wearing a T-shirt or an armband as a symbolic expression is a protected right of minors. The decision in the *Gillman* case in 2008 upholds the precedent set by *Tinker* in 1965. Clothing, stickers, and armbands are all symbolic expression and as such are protected under the First Amendment, provided students do not disrupt school functions. Therefore, schools should not regulate free speech and should promote the exchange of ideas, as was the intent of the delegates of the Constitutional Convention. Also in 2008, an Illinois student was allowed to wear a T-shirt on which the words "Be Happy, Not Gay" were printed to an event promoting tolerance. The student filed suit when he was told he would not be allowed to wear the T-shirt to the event. The case was *Nuxoll v. Indian Prairie School District 204*. The 2008 U.S. Seventh Circuit Court of Appeals decision upheld the student's right to freedom of speech. His protest, it was decided, would not substantially disrupt the educational purpose of the event. Students on both side of an issue have the right to free expression.

Political Persuasion

Americans are free to attempt to persuade each other through speeches, conversation, and debate. Debate is a major part of most elections for governmental office. If citizens fulfill their responsibility to vote their conscience, the officials in office truly represent the constituency. Minors begin to practice participating in the election process in school. Students elect candidates from among their classmates to represent the student body to the administration. It should be a priority that students are able to express their political understanding and beliefs in school. The more

During student government elections, this boy gives his vote.

school officials suppress free expression in the classroom, the harder it will be for students to face real political problems outside the school.

Does censoring students from wearing politically themed clothing protect and promote life, liberty, and the pursuit of happiness? Schools must teach students to be free citizens who participate in their government. By denying students this expression, schools are in fact teaching students not to aspire to the expectations of the Constitution.

45

By oppressing free speech, schools are saying that the opinions and thoughts they have regarding a particular election are not valid and have no place in school.

Equal Access Act

According to the Equal Access Act, a federal law passed in 1984, public schools must also provide some time and a place for student meetings during nonclassroom time. Schools cannot discriminate on the basis of the "religious, political, philosophical, or other content of the speech

Students gather outside Clear Lake High School near Houston, Texas, for morning prayers.

at such meetings." Thus, the rights of all students to gather and meet according to their interests are protected. Exceptions can be made if the meetings cause substantial disruption to the educational mission of the school.

Surprisingly, given the long history of religious institutions censoring the public, religious groups in the United States are one of the strongest proponents of protecting student free speech and the Equal Access Act.

In 1981, in *Widmar v. Vincent*, the Supreme Court overturned the University of Missouri at Kansas City's (UMKC) decision to restrict stu-

WIDMAR V. VINCENT

In *Widmar v. Vincent*, the Supreme Court ruled that the University of Missouri at Kansas City's policy to stop religious groups from meeting on campus violated the principle that any regulation of speech should be content-neutral. Accordingly, school administrators could prohibit groups from meeting on campus, but they could not single out any one type of group. By prohibiting only religious groups from meeting, the university was violating the First Amendment. The question of what is protected under the First Amendment in a public space keeps popping up in courtrooms across the country. In *Widmar* the case revolved around denying a space to certain groups. Some cases involve denying public space for display or demonstration purposes. The state or government must not interfere with each individual's right to worship under any religion they choose. In one court case a monument in a courthouse of the Ten Commandments from the Bible was ruled as a violation of the First Amendment since it served to advocate for one religion.

dent religious groups from meeting on campus. Justice Lewis Powell wrote in the Court's decision, "Here UMKC has discriminated against student groups and speakers based on their desire to use a generally open forum to engage in religious worship and discussion. These are forms of speech and association protected by the First Amendment."

By discriminating against a group based solely on its religious affiliation, the school violated the group's First Amendment rights. If the school had discriminated against groups because of their lack of particular religious affiliation, that would also have been a violation of the First Amendment.

Separation of Church and State

According to the principle of separation of church and state, the government may not promote or deny any one religion. All citizens, including minors, have the right to choose and practice any religion—or none. The courts have consistently protected the rights of religious groups to meet on campus. When Bridget Mergens, a student in a Nebraska high school, wanted to form a Christian club, the school administration denied her request. The Supreme Court overruled the school's decision in 1990. Justice Sandra Day O'Connor stated, "Although a school may not itself lead or direct a religious club, a school that permits a student-initiated religious club to meet after school, just as it permits any other student group to do, does not convey a message of state approval or endorsement of the particular religion." Under the law, the school in

U.S. District Judge Sarah Evans Barker agreed that the placement of a Ten Commandments monument in a public space did indeed violate the First Amendment. Workers here removed the monument.

Nebraska would have to accept a religious student club the same way it would accept a Republican or Democratic student club.

Student Rights

Students have other religious rights protected by the First Amendment when they are in school. For example, students may wear a cross, a Star of David, or any other religious piece of jewelry. Recently, a court ruled in favor of a student whose school district wanted her to remove a tattoo of a cross on her hand.

The First Amendment gives citizens the rights to express themselves through speech, religion, and the press. It is the very protection of the First Amendment that allows students to address the courts regarding possible violations of their rights, by protecting the individual's rights to seek redress of grievances by the government.

WHAT DO YOU THINK?

Are Americans' rights dependent upon their beliefs?

Should the content of student journalists' articles be changed or censored? Do adult journalists get to write whatever they want?

Should students be permitted to stage silent protests in school even if teachers or administrators think the protest is disruptive to the classroom?

Should protests that infringe on the rights of others be permitted?

What do you think President Eisenhower meant when he wrote, "Don't join the book burners"?

Students Silenced!!!

Dr. Dixon, Provost and VP of Academic Affairs, has decided to silence The Gramblinite with a suspension. The staff members of The Gramblinite do understand the need to limit errors in the paper, but a "suspension" is another form of censorship. That is a violation of the First Amendment that allows the Freedom of the Press.

The administration is using the Hosty v. Carter case in Illinois as a lame-brained attempt to prove they are legally right. DO NOT LISTEN!!!

That case involved high school students, which is ENTIRELY different from collegiate papers. For proof, log onto http://www.splc.org and do a site search for it.

CENSORSHIP WILL NOT BE TOLERATED!!!

Chapter 4

The main problem when dealing with issues of students' rights is the question of maturity. Freedom of speech comes with responsibilities that minors are not yet prepared to hold. Even adults sometimes mistake freedom of speech for the freedom to say whatever they want whenever they want. How can a minor with very little experience in society be expected to understand the fine line between what is legally free speech and what infringes on the rights of his or her fellow students?

Not every claim of First Amendment protection is legitimate, especially when the claim for protection involves an infringement of the rights of others. There will always be restrictions on what people can and cannot say. Students are minors and are not able to determine for themselves all consequences of their actions; so parents and schools must censor them when necessary. Therefore, students should be restrained if their actions disrupt the educational purposes of the classroom. A student who violates another's rights should also be restrained. To call such restraint censorship is to distort the meaning of both words.

The editor of the Grambling State University newspaper holds a leaflet posted around campus to protest the administration's bid to cease publication of the student-run paper.

Speech and Press

When Matthew Fraser stood in front of his classmates and used offensive language, it was the administration's decision that he be suspended. The Supreme Court upheld this decision for several reasons. First, Matthew understood that his speech was lewd and that he could be punished for continuing. Second, his speech violated school policies on obscene language. Third, he caused some disruption during the assembly. The decision in *Fraser* determined that the school officials were correct in censoring the student for his inappropriate speech. Chief Justice Burger said in his written opinion, "Under the First Amendment, the use of an offensive form of expression may not be prohibited to adults making what the speaker considers a political point, but it does not follow that the same latitude must be permitted to children in a public school. It is a highly appropriate function of public school education to prohibit the use of vulgar and offensive terms in public discourse." Fraser knew his speech was questionable and still used the offensive language.

No Free Press

Less than twenty years after the *Tinker* decision, which granted First Amendment rights to students, the Supreme Court's decision in *Hazelwood* (1988) declared that students do not have protection under the First Amendment when writing for school-sponsored newspapers. According to the *Hazelwood* decision, school officials have the right to censor school papers. The Court decided that school officials are able

to censor student newspapers if they have not been set up as public forums.

In *Hazelwood*, the justices based their decision on several factors. First, the

> ## DID YOU KNOW?
> A student publication can be sued for libel. Libel is the publication of a false statement that damages a person's reputation. Under the law, a person who has been libeled can sue for monetary compensation. With freedom comes responsibility.

court reasoned that the articles were written as part of a journalism class—in which case the teacher and principal maintain full authority over final publication of all articles. Second, the Court, in agreement with the principal, decided that the two articles were inappropriate for a younger audience. Third, they agreed that if the articles did not meet the expectations of the classroom, they did not need be printed in the paper. Thus, the decision to censor the articles was based on both the quality of the articles and their appropriateness within the confines of the classroom. The teacher in a journalism class has a duty to correct the inappropriateness and direct his or her students in a better direction.

Offensive Clothing

Schools must keep peace within the classroom by censoring speech that is disruptive or infringes on a classmate's rights. For example, a student was suspended for wearing a jacket with a Confederate flag on the sleeve. Because the school had had a history of violence related to the display of the Confederate flag, the Supreme Court upheld the decision of the school to censor the student. The case, *Phillips v. Anderson County School District* was brought before the

This student fought for his right to symbolic expression.

Supreme Court in 1997. The Court's decision declared that when a student does something to incite violence, it should be stopped. Once outside the school, the student would be able to wear the jacket. Some schools have dealt with the problem of disruptive clothing by requiring students to wear uniforms.

It is the purpose of schools to teach children to be good citizens. In the interest of the students, a school may choose to censor behavior that restricts the rights of the students. Students should not have to listen to speech that is vulgar or lewd, be exposed to objectionable journalism, or be forced to watch as someone celebrates a symbol that is offensive to some.

Political Rights

While students should be expected to participate in the election of student body representatives and should be able to express themselves when they think a policy needs to be changed, there are

appropriate ways in which to do so. When a student in a Michigan high school wanted to change his school's tardy policy, it was suggested that he make his proposals to the student senate. Instead, he wrote a three-page letter in which he described the policy. The letter, which included name-calling and lewd and vulgar language, was read aloud during lunch period by the author to students who by the very fact that they had lunch during this period were forced to listen to his speech. After receiving complaints from various students, the school suspended the author of the letter for ten days. Had he followed the policy for getting his voice heard, he would not have been suspended. Instead he raised his disagreement with a school policy to the level of verbal assault.

Rudeness Follows You Everywhere

In a similar case, a student named Avery Doninger and her mother sued the girl's school, Lewis S. High School in Burlington, Connecticut, for violation of her First Amendment rights after she was disqualified from running for senior class secretary. Avery posted vulgar and misleading comments on her blog with the intention of stirring up trouble for school administrators. Avery was unhappy that an event called Jamfest was being postponed because the opening of the new auditorium was delayed. So Avery and a few members of the student council drafted an e-mail urging its readers to call the district superintendent, Paula Schwartz, and entreat her to hold

Avery Doninger used her personal blog to express her opinions about what was going on at school. Her use of name calling may prevent this speech from being protected by the First Amendment.

Jamfest as scheduled. The e-mail also urged readers to forward it to other people. School principal Karissa Niehoff and the superintendent received many calls after the e-mail went out. Avery claimed that the principal was canceling Jamfest as a result of these calls. Niehoff said that she was concerned with the fact that student council members had resorted to an e-mail rather than following proper channels, as members were expected to demonstrate "good citizenship" at all times.

Schools across the country are dealing with increasing bullying and cyberbullying episodes.

Instead of following proper student council procedures, Avery posted an abusive rant on her public blog. In this entry, she called the staff of the central office rude names and continued to ask people to call the superintendent to urge the school not to cancel Jamfest. As a result, the principal declined to give Avery permission to run for student council again. Avery and her mother sued the school district. As of 2011, *Doninger v. Niehoff et al* was in appeal in the U.S. Second Circuit Court of

Appeals in New York, though no court date had been set. Each lower court that has heard the case has ruled that the school did not violate Avery's rights as she did not follow the proper procedures as a member of the student council.

Avery's problem is that she resorted to name calling and urged a disruption of the business of the school over a misunderstanding. In the end, Jamfest took place just a few weeks after it was originally scheduled.

For a Pennsylvania teen in 2008, wearing a T-shirt with the image of a gun on the front along with the words Volunteer Homeland Security was also considered unacceptable. (The words Special Issue Resident Lifetime License—United States Terrorist Hunting Permit—Permit No. 91101—Gun Owner—No Bag Limit were written on the back.) When asked by the school to turn the T-shirt inside-out, the boy, believing his right to free speech was being infringed upon, refused and was suspended for two days. The student sued the school district claiming his rights had been violated. In *Miller v. Penn Manor School District et al*, the Pennsylvania Eastern District Court agreed with the school administrators. The law allows for "restriction of speech that promotes illegal behavior or communicates the threat of violence."

DID YOU KNOW?

According to Federal Bureau of Investigation crime statistics, there were 7,783 hate crimes reported in 2008. Over 16 percent of these crimes were motivated by religious bias.

There are times when certain behavior is not acceptable. Schools have a duty to protect students from any speech that could incite violence. The teen wore an image of a gun coupled with words that express the desire to kill human beings. What other option did the school have?

Students and Religion

A California teen was suspended for wearing a T-shirt that had the words "Be ashamed our school embraced what God has condemned" on the front and "Homosexuality is ew shameful—Romans 1:27" on the back. He wore this T-shirt on an organized Day of Silence that was designed to encour-

This student from New Jersey was suspended from his school for wearing inappropriate attire.

age tolerance in a school that was having difficulties between students on both sides of the issue. Opponents claimed that the wearing of the T-shirt was done to cause disruption. In the 2008 case, *Harper v. Poway Unified School District,* the student claimed his rights had been violated. However, both the U.S. Ninth Circuit Court and U.S. Ninth Circuit Court of Appeals upheld the decision of the school to suspend the teen.

Free exercise of religion is guaranteed by the Constitution and the Bill of Rights. Thus, any public school–sanctioned event cannot promote one religion over any other. In 2002, Boca Raton Community High School allowed students to paint murals in the hallways as part of a school beautification project. One group painted a mural with many Christian symbols, including the cross, and a verse from the Bible that contained the words Jesus and God. When the school asked the students to remove the religious symbols, one student filed a lawsuit against the school for violation of her First Amendment rights of free expression of religion. The courts, however, agreed with the school. This was a school-sanctioned event, and according to the *Hazelwood* decision, an administrator can censor speech if there is educational merit.

In the Wake of Violence

Columbine High School was the location of one of the worst school shootings in history; twelve students and one teacher were killed. Soon after the shootings, the school allowed students to paint tiles to be hung in the hallways. There were some stipulations: the tiles were not to have religious symbols, obscene or offensive language, names or initials of students, or any reference to the attack. Several students' tiles were rejected because they violated the stipulations. The students sued for violation of free expression of religion. The U.S. Tenth Circuit Court of Appeals in 2004 sided with the school in the ruling of *Fleming v. Jefferson County School District R-1 R*. The tiles in this case represented

Police respond to the violence at Columbine High School on April 20, 1999.

speech endorsed by the school. The messages would be an expression of the school. Therefore, the school was within bounds to set limitations on the type of speech allowed.

In this case, the school's objective was not to create a memorial to the massacre but to help maintain the school's objective as a place of learning. "School officials made a concerted effort to change the appearance of the building to avoid incorporating sensory cues that could reactivate memories of the attack." Further disruptions to the school would not be prudent for students who had recently suffered so much.

COLUMBINE MASSACRE

On a Tuesday in April 1999, twelve students were murdered at Columbine High School and over twenty-one students injured when two students opened fire on their classmates. Despite the many signs that the two boys, Eric Harris and Dylan Klebold, were becoming very violent, it was a shock to the students when the attack started. The case sparked debate about student rights, gun control, and even the use of prescription medication in mental health care.

Schools protect all students. If a person's religious point of view begins to restrict the rights of others and cause disruption in class, then the school is correct in censoring that expression. Any speech, political or religious, offensive or just, must not restrict the rights of other students in the school.

WHAT DO YOU THINK?

Do you think that the same rules about speech and clothing should apply to minority group students and majority group students?

If a symbol or a slogan has a positive meaning for one group of people and a negative meaning for another, who gets to decide whether it is permitted?

Do you think Avery Doninger should have been able to write whatever she wanted to on her blog? What if what she said in

the blog was completely true? What if what she said in the blog was not true?

Should schoolchildren have the same rights and privileges that adults have?

Do you think teachers and school administrators should have the right to determine whether or not a speech is lewd or vulgar?

Early democracies granted free speech only to certain landowning men. In historic terms, the right to free speech in a democratic society is a relatively new phenomenon. For United States citizens, free speech is protected in the Bill of Rights, the first ten amendments to the Constitution. In the more than 220 years since the First Amendment was ratified, court cases specifically addressing free speech of students have been tried only in the last fifty years. The rise of social media, cyberbullying, and violence in schools in the last fifteen years highlights even more issues to be considered in the debate of student rights.

Students in middle and high schools are considered minors. Historically, it fell to parents and school administrators to regulate the behavior of minors. The Court first upheld the right to symbolic expression in the case of Mary Beth and John Tinker. Symbolic expression can be a button or a T-shirt with a slogan, a belt buckle or an armband. This book has presented both sides of the debate over student free speech. Should students be given protection under the First Amendment?

Students, teachers, and administrators have many issues to think about in today's diverse classrooms.

Do you think that students should have the full protection under the First Amendment?

Think over some of the cases that were decided in favor of free speech for students. Think about some of the cases in which the courts decided in favor of censorship. Were the court decisions right? Would the decisions have been different if the setting of each case had not been a school? Would adults have been given the same decisions by the courts? What might be different about each case because of the school setting?

WHAT DO YOU THINK?

The debate over student rights has two sides. Have you taken a side?

Should there be different laws for minors and adults? Why or why not?

What does good citizenship mean?

Do you think individual rights outweigh those of the group? Why or why not?

Is there a difference between protesting and hate speech?

What does it mean to have free speech?

Timeline

399 BCE — Socrates is tried for corrupting the youth of Athens.

1215 — King John is forced to sign the Magna Carta.

1517 — Martin Luther nails the *Ninety-five Theses* to the door of the Wittenburg Church, sparking the Reformation.

1620 — Plymouth Colony is the first Pilgrim colony established in the New World.

1633 — Galileo is tried for heresy for supporting the Copernican theory of the planets.

1776 — New World colonies draft the Declaration of Independence to separate from the British crown.

1787 — Delegates from colonies meet in Philadelphia, Pennsylvania, to draft Constitution.

1789 — First Congress signs the Bill of Rights into law.

1870 — Fifteenth Amendment to the Constitution outlaws denying the right to vote to people based on race and color.

1917 — Espionage Act is adopted.

1918 — Alien and Sedition Acts are adopted.

1920 — American Civil Liberties Union is founded.

1920 — Nineteenth Amendment to the Constitution grants women right to vote.

1948 — The United Nations proclaims the Universal Declaration of Human Rights, including the right to free speech.

1968 — Supreme Court grants students protection under the First Amendment in the decision in *Tinker v. Des Moines*.

1981 — Supreme Court overturns University of Missouri at Kansas City's decision to restrict student religious groups from meeting on campus in *Widmar v. Vincent*.

1983 — Supreme Court sides with the school over a student's right to use vulgar language during a speech in *Bethel School District v. Fraser*.

1984 — Equal Access Act passes federally.

1988 — Administration is granted the right to censor student writings in school paper in *Hazelwood School District v. Kuhlmeier*.

1990 — Supreme Court rules in favor of a student's right to form a religious group in *Westside School District v. Mergens*.

1997 — Supreme Court upholds decision to censor symbolic expression in cases such as *Phillips v. Anderson County School District* in which there was a history of violence.

1997 — Supreme Court unanimously supports extension of First Amendment rights to the Internet in *Reno v. American Civil Liberties Union*.

1999 — Massacre at Columbine High School.

2003 — United States Congress requires public schools and libraries to install web filtering software as condition to receiving federal funding in *United States v. American Library Association*.

2004 — Student journalist rights upheld in decision of *Dean v. Utica Community*.

2004 — Columbine memorial tiles deemed expression of the school rather than individual student artists in *Fleming v. Jefferson County School District R-1 R*.

2007 — Students behavior off school grounds still falls under school authority according to the decision of *Morse v. Frederick*.

2008 — School board ordered to reverse decision to punish student for wearing a T-shirt to support homosexual friends in *Gillman v. School Board for Holmes Country Florida et al*.

2008 — Grossmont Union High School repeals its decision to keep students from wearing buttons or T-shirts that express their opinion of Proposition 8 in California.

2008 — Student punishment for T-shirt promoting violence is upheld by court in *Miller v. Penn Manor School District et al*.

2008 — Teen suspended in California for wearing a T-shirt intended to cause disruption in *Harper v. Poway Unified School District*.

2010 — Voting results for Proposition 8 ballet in California overturned by Justice Walker.

2011 — Decision on the *Doninger v. Niehoff et al* appeal pending.

Glossary

allege—To charge or accuse, with or without evidence.

amendment—An addition or change to a written document; specifically, the U.S. Constitution.

Bill of Rights—A list of rights recognized in law. In the U.S. Constitution, the Bill of Rights refers to the first ten amendments, which enumerate powers denied to the government and list rights reserved to the individual states or to the American people.

blasphemy—Deliberate insulting irreverence toward God, specific religious beliefs, or anything else considered sacred.

censorship—The silencing or suppressing of expression considered objectionable. Censorship comes in many forms and in many arenas: moral, military, political, religious, and corporate. Things censored may include books, films, art, speech, demonstrations, and clothing.

civics—The study of citizenship and civic affairs, especially in a particular society.

civil rights—Rights of citizens. The civil rights movement in America centered on establishing equal rights for all citizens regardless of race.

constitution—A document that outlines fundamental rules and establishes understandings by which a state, country, or other organization is governed. Capitalized, the word refers to the Constitution of the United States of America.

copyright—The legal right to reproduce, publish, or distribute material.

Declaration of Independence—The document that formally proclaimed the political separation of America's thirteen British colonies from Great Britain.

forum—A public meeting place or medium for the open discussion of subjects of public interest.

free speech—The right to expression.

heresy—An opinion, belief, or action that directly opposes the established understanding. Usually refers to opposition to an established religious belief system.

inquisition—A formal inquiry; an interrogation. The Inquisition, a panel of ecclesiastical judges within the Roman Catholic Church, was established by Pope Gregory IX in 1232 to eradicate heresy and try heretics.

Jim Crow laws— A set of laws that promoted the segregation of African Americans from the white community. These laws were created after African Americans gained full U.S. citizenship.

lewd—Something offensive, especially in a sexually offensive way.

liberties—Freedoms.

Magna Carta—A thirteenth-century document that confirmed specific rights of English noblemen and commoners and placed distinct limits on the power of the crown.

obstruction—Something that blocks; a barricade.

proposition—In legal terms, a proposal that if accepted by vote will become law.

ratification—The act of making something legally binding, formalizing.

redress—To set something right, to fix.

republican—Pertaining to the republic, a form of government in which the power belongs to the people who elect representatives.

symbolic expression—The legal definition of "symbolic expression" or "symbolic speech" is any means of nonverbal communication. Clothing can sometimes be considered symbolic speech.

vulgar—Explicit and offensive.

Find Out More

Books

Frohnmayer, John. *Out of Tune: Listening to the First Amendment*. Nashville, TN: Freedom Forum First Amendment Center, 1994.

Lewis, Anthony. *Freedom for the Thought That We Hate: A Biography of the First Amendment*. New York: Basic Books, 2007.

Tedford, Thomas L., and Dale A. Herbeck. *Freedom of Speech in the United States*. State College, PA: Strata, 2005.

Websites

American Civil Liberties Union
www.aclu.org/

British Library, Great Treasures, the Magna Carta
www.bl.uk/treasures/magnacarta/

Charters of Freedom
www.archives.gov/exhibits/charters/

First Amendment Center
www.firstamendmentcenter.org/

Freedom Forum
www.freedomforum.org/

Justia: Law and Legal Information for Lawyers, Students, Business and the Public

www.justia.com/

National Archives

www.archives.gov/

Open Jurist: Making the Laws of the Land Accessible to the People of the Land

http://openjurist.org/

Student Press Law Center

www.splc.org/

Index
Page numbers in boldface are illustrations.

About the Author

Aubrey Hicks received a bachelor's degree in English from Moravian College and a master's degree in library and information science from the University of Illinois at Urbana-Champaign. She has worked as a reference librarian and in administration at a large publishing house. Currently Ms. Hicks is an assistant director for a university research center on governance. Ms. Hicks loves reading anything that she can get her hands on.